From Trinity to Treanmanagh
further reminiscences

Pat in Kerry, c 1953

Pat in Kerry, c 2000

Pat in Treanmanagh, County Kerry

Patrick Melia

FROM TRINITY TO TREANMANAGH
further reminiscences

ARLEN
HOUSE

FROM TRINITY TO TREANMANAGH
further reminiscences

is published in 2014 by
ARLEN HOUSE
42 Grange Abbey Road
Baldoyle
Dublin 13, Ireland
Phone/Fax: 353 86 8207617
Email: arlenhouse@gmail.com
www.arlenhouse.blogspot.com

Distributed internationally by
SYRACUSE UNIVERSITY PRESS
621 Skytop Road, Suite 110
Syracuse, NY 13244–5290
Phone: 315–443–5534/Fax: 315–443–5545
Email: supress@syr.edu
www.syracuseuniversitypress.syr.edu

ISBN 978–1–85132–085–1, paperback

Typesetting ¦ Arlen House

Special thanks to Fiona McCormack, Lissy Walsh, Brian Melia, Nina Finn-Kelcey, Poppy Melia, Pauline Bewick, Conor Mulvihill, Alan McWeeney, Betty O'Shea, Eliza O'Shea, Regine Bartsch, Mike O'Neill, Aran Mulvihill and Adam Mulvihill.

Contents

Pat Melia, c. 1964

From Trinity to Treanmanagh
Further Reminiscences

Pat and his mother Edith

Paddy and Edith Melia, Pat's parents

My Father, Paddy Melia

My father was intended for the priesthood, at least that was his mother's view of the matter. The first step was entry into Maynooth Clerical College. Here he studied Greek and Latin, and most importantly, Divinity. By his own account he had little interest in these subjects. The only such matter that he showed to me was a sentence written using the Greek alphabet which he clearly enjoyed writing with his walking stick on the strand at Sandymount, Dublin. I do not recall whether he gave us a translation of the sentence, but rather think not.

He finished his BA in Classical Languages and graduated from Maynooth, but he was not ordained. His own explanation for this failure was that he and the Maynooth hierarchy did not get on well together. His version was that he and some of his friends had taken refuge behind a hedge and lit up their pipes for an illicit smoke. At the time clerical students were not permitted to smoke, and my father described to me how the Maynooth clerics pursued him and his friends:

> we saw them cross the hedges and ditches and run across the fields towards us, their gowns flying out behind them.

Next morning they had to appear before members of the hierarchy. My father forestalled any disciplinary action against him by immediately resigning. Then it was the train to Roscommon and life there back in the family home. His father styled himself a merchant and ran a thriving grocery shop as well as importing tea into most of the West of Ireland.

The family was large and apparently indolent. Eddie though, called after his father, was a brilliant Latin scholar at Castleknock College, coming first out of all Ireland. There were eleven brothers and sisters, who included two nuns, but otherwise none of them took up any regular work. My father joined this enclave of unemployment.

After a year or two a breakthrough occurred – he joined the Medical School of University College, Dublin. In order to attend the lectures he entered the Jesuit Hostel in Hatch Street. Not without a certain pride my father confided to me that at this time parents who considered that their offspring needed special disciplinary supervision were found places in the Hatch Street Hostel, to the extent that it had jocularly earned the nickname of Inebriates' Hall.

Nevertheless, and without undue delay, he qualified in medicine and found a post where he obtained the required practical experience to become a fully registered Medical Practitioner. This he did in the hospital at Canterbury in Kent. Here he worked hard for long hours and enjoyed the experience. He had some leisure and in summer watched cricket at the county ground. He particularly admired the elegant batsmanship of the left hander Frank Wolley.

On his way back to Ireland after completing his internship he stopped off in London and spent all the money he had earned. He frequented the Café Royal and commented that 'the girls had terrible queer hair-dos'.

At this point it seems likely that my father had sown his wild oats, and decided to settle in his native Roscommon. He went into partnership with a local GP. There followed two incidents which persuaded him to emigrate to Britain. He was called out to see a sick patient. It was 1922 and motor cars were a rarity and my father used a hired car. The driver was so excited by the drama of what he perceived to be an emergency call that he rounded the first corner that they came to at such a speed that he overturned the car, throwing himself and my father out onto the road. The next incident also featured a sick call. On this occasion my father's partner arrived at the home of the patient and dismissed the relatives from the sick room. After a lengthy wait nothing was heard and the relatives decided to investigate. They found the partner fast asleep in bed beside the patient. My father found such mercurial behaviour hard to accept and set off to find a more temperate environment.

The best jobs had already been taken by the English doctors and the Irish emigrant doctors took what was left over – which was working with Welsh coal miners, often migrants themselves, living in the deep valleys where the coal mines were sunk. The valleys were dominated by slag heaps and ugly railways which bore the wagons that were loaded with freshly dug coal. It was in these valleys that my father worked. The patients paid in tontines, a penny a week, a simple insurance scheme which suited the miners and my father.

Above the coal pits were some farms and above this moorland. My father used to go shooting with some friends and soon he took up golf. He rented a gaunt rambling house. His next move was surprising but characteristic.

He met Edith Mary Inglis at the house of his partner. When, after a short stay, she returned to Liverpool he noticed that her thank you letter was left lying on the hall table. He pocketed it and was in possession of her address which he had been too shy to ask for. Now he lost no time in making use of it. He wrote to Edith and asked her out and he travelled the twenty odd miles to Liverpool to meet her. They went to the theatre. In the interval my mother playfully suggested that to drink he should have a ginger beer and she a ginger ale. He agreed on this occasion, but was careful in future to firmly order a glass of whiskey, his much preferred drink.

Fairly soon they got married. They were a case of opposites getting on well together. My mother was talkative and friendly, my father though easygoing, was apt to be silent and retiring. My mother once commented to me that many of the young men who were her contemporaries had been killed in the Great War. Perhaps this was a factor in her choice of an Irish Catholic as her husband. In the event my mother converted from her native Anglicanism to Catholicism, she said to placate my father's mother.

Children came along: Edward William was the first, then John Patrick who died in infancy. I was the replacement. Probably my mother's confidence was dented by the death of her second born. My nurse was Rose. Unlike Bill's nurse who was fully trained, Rose was a country girl, and I loved her above all.

Bill and Pat Melia, with their father Paddy

Back row: Herbert Griffiths (friend), Bill Melia and Milo Waldren (relative and sports reporter for the *Irish Independent).*
Front row: Paddy Melia, Rose Davis (nurse), Pat and Edith Melia

My Childhood

The Convent

When I was five I was sent to the local convent day school. I started off on the wrong foot with the nuns, and never in the five years I was there managed to get onto the desirable correct foot. For instance there was the God in the inkwell debacle. Sister Beginnis, at least I thought that was her name, explained to the class that God was everywhere. I was intrigued by this idea and asked was he even in the inkwell on my desk. To my consternation this enraged Sister Beginnis – she snatched up her ruler and charged through the classroom to administer redemption. Besides myself there was only one other pupil in the class who was a Catholic. The others were mostly Welsh chapel goers.

Philomena's Exit

This was Philomena who left her mouth wide open and stared about vacantly. Philomena and I were to receive Holy Communion, and as a preliminary we had a dry run. Everything was the real thing except that the host was not blessed. Philomena and I kneeled at the altar rail, the priest approached and repeated that we would have the Body and Blood of Christ within us, at which Philomena screamed and ran out of the chapel.

Unkindly I took comfort in the fact that I was not the only one who could screw up the ceremony, like I did with my navy-blue short trousers on Communion Day. The nuns had stipulated that all the First Communicants should have a white top and bottom. My mother, however, decided that navy-blue trousers would be acceptable, especially as they would only be worn on the one occasion. How wrong she was! Sister Beginnis was outraged and I bore the brunt of her grumblings for many a day.

At last after five years my ordeal, as I felt it to be, was over, and I was enrolled at Arnold House, the Junior School which was the preparatory for the King's School in Chester. Miss Smith was the mistress in charge of Form One and she managed it with serenity. Everything was orderly and sensible and it was a pleasure to be there.

Getting there, however, was not so easy. First I had to catch the Summerhill bus to Wrexham – this took a quarter of an hour and was followed by a walk across Wrexham to catch another bus to Chester which took half an hour to reach and a walk across the town to complete the journey. But my mother thought it was worth it to go to a good school and I agreed with her.

Rose, my nanny, got married when I was five. Her husband was Stan Davies who drove the number ten crane at Brynbo steelworks. With it he collected the white-hot ingots from the open hearth furnaces and trundelled them over to the rolling mills where the foreman George Maelor saw that they were flattened out to a more manageable size.

After Rose and Stan were married in Brinbo Church they drove to the wedding breakfast with me sitting between them so that I would not feel ousted; kindness indeed!

My mother enjoyed my company more now that I was a little older and could take part in a conversation. My father looked after the practice: surgery at about nine o'clock, then house calls at Summerhill and the surrounding villages: Gwersylt, The Moss, Pentre Broughton, Brynteg and so on, dinner at half past one, a nap for my father after dinner in the armchair in front of the fire; and then a walk with my mother – the dogs and, if we were not in school, Bill or I might join them. Home for tea, then the evening surgery.

My father enjoyed the independence of general practice as it was then: he delivered babies, set fractures, pulled teeth and was a medical Jack of all trades. My mother did the secretarial work; that done she would get out her bicycle and ride on it downhill three miles to Wrexham to do the shopping. There were no refrigerators in those days so shopping was a daily affair. The milk had a status of its own, the farm at the bottom of the fields had a pony and cart in which the farmer brought it up and delivered it from house to house around the village. In the evening my mother and whatever children were about walked down by the Pissel style to the farm with our cans and had them filled by Mrs Mathias, the farmer's wife, with the fresh evening's milking.

Once in Wrexham my mother bought the shopping in the town and met my father who relieved her of the heavy bags which she had hanging from the handlebars and then she cycled back to Summerhill. But the job my mother liked best was coaching me and helping me with my homework. She was a school teacher before their marriage and was very good at it. Her special subject was geography.

She was a Liverpudlian and had attended the University there. The family was originally from Aberdeen and her father had moved to Liverpool as a young man and became apprenticed to a marine engineer. Her brother went to Jesus College Oxford and studied history. After University, Edith taught at Giggleswick College in the Northern Pennines until the time of her marriage. They all lived together in a house in Liverpool, though with the father being away at sea and Edith and Willy being at University, there must have been times when there was only the mother at home.

The house that our family lived in at Summerhill was in East Denbighshire, now called Clwyd. It was set above the road. There were two roads: Top road and Bottom road. We were on Top road. Above us there was a small disused slag heap over which a number of fowl walked and clucked.

Then began the village proper which consisted of irregular small terraces dotted about, seemingly at random. The village had been built towards the end of the nineteenth century in order to accommodate workers for the Summerhill Colliery. This was now defunct, the coal seams having been exhausted. The inhabitants had stayed on to not waste the houses. They continued working in the pits such as Gresford, Llay and New Broughton which still had coal to be mined.

The district was a hilly one. Summerhill was perched on a ridge and the disused colliery and slag heap occupied the summit, together with the ruined miners' institute and the giant fan which in its day ventilated the coal mine, the remains of which were mostly underground. There was a level patch where we played cricket. Eric Williams used to come thundering in over the slag ashes and deliver his deadly fast bowling from beyond the willow herbs, across a path which straddled the ridge and descended steeply to a valley on the western side where there was a railway line. This joined some other lines and swept down behind a slag heap in the direction of Wrexham.

There was also an abandoned railway tunnel passing under the Summerhill ridge and emerging a hundred yards or so in a little wooded valley below our house. This used to connect the Brynmally colliery and the main line at Gwersylt. To the north was the Brynbo valley in the depths of which was the steelworks with its glowing ingots and showers of red hot slag.

Bill and Pat c. 1939 with the local woodcutter and his assistants

School Days

My own connection with the river – it was the Welsh Dee – came when I was twelve years old and at school in Chester. A cox was needed. I seemed to be the only one able to swim, so I got the job. My training began with an outing in a so-called tub, which was broad in the beam. Two older oarsmen crewed it and I sat on the floorboards between the coach's legs and steered under his supervision. Mr Charles, the coach, was said to have an Oxford accent, though at the time I was unable to make any distinction on such a matter.

The cox's principal task was to steer the boat. He also gave orders passed to him by the oarsman in front of him, the 'stroke' who was the Captain of the boat. The orders were given in a stereotyped manner, and most important, a loud voice. To start off, like this: 'Come forward, are you ready? Paddle; and to stop "Easy All"'.

Mr Charles wore, under his jacket, a green waistcoat with white spots. He organized the House Fours. The Fours were long, thin racing boats with four oarsmen and a cox. The school was divided into four houses and these would race each other; Lindens, Shepherds, Falls and Evans.

The start of the race was about a mile upstream from the boathouses, near the church at Boughton, St Paul's. The course swung about and ended by the bandstand just above the weir. Lindens, my team, won on this occasion and I congratulated myself for steering onto the inside of the bends. Mr Charles presented each of the winning oarsmen and the cox with a silver medal which made us hugely pleased.

Our next venture took us right up the river in practice for the Head of the River Race. The river curved up alongside the meadows, then along some lengthy straits to Heron's Bridge and further into hills and bends and woods three miles up to the start of the Head of the River Race at Eccleston Ferry. We were rowing downriver one evening on the strait above Boughton, St Paul's, when the outrigger splashed in the spray, the boat lifted in the water and the spray turned salty as we hit the incoming tide.

The King's School did not have an eight at that time so we joined forces with the Grosvenor Rowing Club with whom we already shared a boathouse. We overtook two boats in our descent which was the most we could reasonably expect. So the Head of the River Race was over for the year. It had been in abeyance for several years and this was the first one to be held since the war.

The school occupied buildings in and around Abbey Square. This was reached by passing under Abbeygate. To the left in the near corner was the Bishop's Palace, to the right was the Choir School; the boys wore red caps. Most of the King's School buildings were to the right. Opposite was the little road that led down past Mr Bayte's house and thence to the city walls. Mr Bayte was the Head Master, he spoke with an aristocratic drawl, his presence was riveting but soon he went off to join the army and his place was taken by B.T. Williams who taught French. B.T. also had an arresting voice which commanded instant attention, but unlike Mr Bayte he was not intimidating and it was possible to have an interesting conversation with him in the classroom. There were a variety of games such as gymnastics but above all I liked cricket. I played for the colt teams and eventually played for the Second Eleven and was chosen to be the wicket keeper. The matches started in the morning and the dew was on the ground. We had a new ball for each match and it swung for the fast bowlers and entered the wicket keeper's gloves with a satisfying thud.

Next Summer I was in the First Eleven. The Captain and Vice Captain had anxious consultations about the large number of byes given away in the previous season. Eventually they approached me and told me that I could have a trial as wicket keeper and would be kept on if I could keep down the large number of byes that my predecessors had conceded. As it turned out I was the goal-keeper type of wicket keeper rather than the rapid fast worker behind the stamps and I did not let any byes go through in the match.

Skiing through the years

Skiing at St Anton, 1952

We are at Calais SNCF. We have just crossed the Channel on this blustery late-winter's day. In the saloon of the ferry boat the cries of 'Porter, Porter' have died down and we are following the porters who carry our bags to the station restaurant. We pass the enormous locomotive standing at the shallow platform snorting steam and bearing the placard 'CB', standing for Calais-Bâle.

I follow John into the station-restaurant; it is small and made of corrugated iron. John orders for both of us: *oeufs en plat.* I had expected something more elaborate, but it is delicious and I am quite happy to let him lead, he has been here before and loves the continent. We board the train. It is about 6p.m. and we settle down for the long overnight journey. The engine gets up steam, great jets suddenly shoot across the platform followed by a long constant billowing cloud emerging through the wheels. Then at last a feeble little piping seeming quite inadequate for the task, and we are off.

John and I were medical students at Trinity College, Dublin and this story begins in 1952, seven years after the end of World War II, when the station restaurant had still to be rebuilt, but first things first: we had a delicious meal. Our train lumbered out of the station. We had a compartment to ourselves but little in the way of comfort, not even couchettes. Eventually the long night was over and we reached Bâle.

John led the way to a comfortable hotel and insisted that we should take showers. I had piled my clothes on a bathroom chair and as I turned on one of the bewildering array of shining taps I sprayed them liberally. I felt rather aggrieved but John poo-pooed my grumbles and we had fresh rolls and coffee for breakfast and marched on for our train to St Anton, the skiing resort which was our destination. The third-class compartment had slatted wooden seats through which the sun shone brightly.

'Haus Mal' where we stayed was on the main street where we shared a room on the top floor. There was a wash stand by each bed with a jug and ewer each and we looked out over the wooden houses across the road behind which towered the magnificent Alps.

We walked up the road to the Gasthof-post for dinner. The dining room was entirely wooden and the waiters wore evening dress. We ate and drank a lot and John talked about the piste. I didn't gain a very clear idea about what this was, other than one might get on it and that it was rather menacing. We walked back under the stars to Haus Mal and I learned that it was the family home of Eddie Mal the champion skier, now the son of the house.

Next morning we donned our skiing outfits. John's was a neat affair with narrow tapering trousers in the new fashion; mine was a pre-war job with voluminous pantaloons tucked into long woolen socks. John studied them doubtfully and eventually pronounced that they were workman-like; and we set out for the *skiplatz* where the newly-arrived skiers congregated. This was presided over by Rudi Mat one of the co-founders of the famous Arlberg Ski School, which we duly joined.

Rudi Mat put me in one of the beginners' classes together with a slender girl of about twelve and a robust little boy of about ten. We put on our skis and trudged off to Nasserein, a small village to the East of St Anton. The two youngsters did fairly well led by our *skilehrer* Otto, who took a very relaxed approach to the proceedings. I had no control whatever over my skis. Instead of traversing the slope I somehow slithered slowly, directly down it, until I fell, which was usually sooner rather than later. This went on for about two days after which I came to the tentative conclusion that I had some irredeemable disorder of my ankles which made it impossible for me to ski. Then there was an unheralded complete change in my legs and I was able to traverse the slope like my young classmates and everyone else, apart from the occasional hopeless cases who lingered at the bottom of most beginners' slopes. I had inadvertently learned to 'edge' my skis correctly. My new-found mobility enabled me to join Otto and the youngsters on some quite ambitious expeditions in the afternoons.

We caught a bus after lunch which wound its way along a snowy path until it stopped at a wooden hut. Here the youngsters and I dismounted at the Waldhaus, put on our skis and used our new-found skills at traversing; and skied, albeit slowly, down through the woods on a path which led back to St Anton. We were surrounded by snowy peaks and forests of pine, and at the head of the valley was the lofty peak of the Pateriol, dominating all.

Well, almost all: John mentioned the Thédansant. For this alluring pursuit John and I had to spruce ourselves up and get a table at the Hôtel Post. There we made our way to the nearest girls' table and each invited a girl to dance. The orchestra was excellent and had been brought up from Vienna for the winter season. It had a repertoire quite different from the Dublin bands: a jauntiness and perky squealing of the clarinet which was quite beguiling.

Our response though was disappointing, partly because we had kept our clumsy ski boots on which must also have struck terror into our partners at the prospect of so much foot trampling. But the girls showed much fortitude and good humour. Eventually we made our way back to Haus Mal, crunching through the new ice and making the snow squeak.

Taking one's skis to be serviced proved to be quite an adventure. The premises where the job was done was a sort of antique cave. The wax on the sole of the ski was melted off by a hot iron and the old wax was replaced by a thick coat of new wax which might be red or it might be silver. Red was for wet sticky snow; silver was for speed. I left my skis in even though neither red nor silver seemed to offer much benefit. The fact was that I had been distracted by something else far more interesting.

Two visitors were staring intently through binoculars up the valley from the steps of the Hôtel Post, and following their line of vision in to the bottom of the pine forest I saw an eagle devouring a baby deer, and he remained at it for three more days, after which we saw him no more. Our own diet shifted to a more danubic one: rice tended to replace potatoes, and delicious cakes – torte – featured for desserts.

We got up early and journeyed to St Christof by cable car. The snow was icy at this early hour, so we propped up our skis and sat on the terrace of a café and drank a café-au-lait until the snow softened. The new girl said to Otto, 'We're just popping off for some yoghurt' to explain the short absence.

The air was crisp and exhilarating and we skied most of the day around that high altitude until a nip of frost reminded us that we must ski home to St Anton. First above the tree line, then through the trees and pistes to the snow round about the huts still full of the summer's hay. Now it was late March and just above the village of St Anton the goats were let out of their hut and frisked about with their bells ringing loudly.

1950: Living and studying in Trinity College, Dublin

1960s: Reading aloud with the family teddy at Heytesbury Lane

Living in College

It was 1952. The season for skiing had passed and it was time to turn to the joys of anatomy, physiology, history and the like. I had moved into rooms in Trinity in New Square with two friends and had settled into a pleasant routine that included study and some, but not too much, recreation. My 'college wives' as they were jocularly called, were slow to leave their beds in the morning so I did not have their company until later in the day. My first engagement was at 9a.m., the lecture in anatomy. I liked particularly Professor Erskine's lecture in neuroanatomy. He used chalks of varying thickness and different colours and by the end of his hour he had built up a work of art on the blackboard.

The weather was mild and after the lecture I made for Number 6 which was the college shop and bought a fresh Vienna loaf and walked with it under my arm. The surplus flour dusted my gown as I made my way in the warm morning air under the campanile back to my rooms for breakfast. Later I would often visit Chris Raphael in his capacious rooms in the Rubrics. He would make toast over a gas fire and we would have coffee together, talking about some flamboyant eccentric we had discovered in college and whose antics we enjoyed. Lunch was generally resolved between buffet in the dining hall and Davy Byrnes. The dining hall was and is an architectural gem, a very large gem. Together with the college chapel it forms one side of Front Square. It is plain but beautifully proportioned, made of light grey stone. Set in its front is a clock whose face is light blue, there is no other decoration.

Davy Byrnes is a different kettle of fish. It is a public house in Duke Street where it is mentioned by James Joyce: Leopold Bloom orders a cheese sandwich and a glass of burgundy, for which he pays '7d, sir'. I order two prawns, an anchovy, a cheese sandwich and a glass of Spatenbrau, for which I pay a couple of shillings. There is much congenial talk. There were lectures in the afternoons not only on medical subjects, but also in the Arts, the thinking in Trinity at that time was that Arts students should have some knowledge of the Sciences and that students of Science should have some knowledge of the Arts; in short they should have a liberal education.

After a year or two there was an exam called Little Go for all students, then in another year or so there was the Pass Arts exam. After that we went on to take specialist examinations.

There were other tasks to occupy us in the afternoons; one was grooming. The highlight as far as this was concerned was the visit to the college

Bath House. This was situated in the Square known as Botany Bay. I do not know how it acquired this raffish name, but I expect that it was due to its secluded position away from the senior members of the college. At this time the central part of the Square had an earthen base, and the other part was planted with hawthorn trees. It was across this we walked from New Square with towels under our arms to the Bath House.

Inside there were about a dozen large porcelain baths, some of them filled and steaming and others already occupied by bathers. All was presided over by a tall college skip. He continued to wear a trilby hat throughout the proceedings and directed one to a full bath and saw that there was a supply of soap. It was luxury indeed, especially because the remainder of the week was spartan. There was no running water in college rooms. There was a tap in New Square from which our skip drew a bucket of water and then it was a matter of using a basin and ewer.

Commons was served at six o'clock in the Dining Hall. Senior members sat at the High Table along with scholars; and undergraduates noisily took their places in the body of the hall. All wore academic gowns which were generally black. A scholar climbed into the pulpit and read the lengthy grace in Latin. Thus fortified we received our meal from the skips who hurried about from table to table. The favourite day for commons was Thursday because this was the day on which pork was served. It was greatly liked because of the crunchy crackling.

To drink we were given jugs of the college beer, which was sour and no one could drink it. But to end on a good note I am glad to say that it has been replaced by good Guinness stout.

I often joined Dan Rogers and Chris Raphael on commons. They were both very amusing. Dan told his stories in a slow drawl; Chris was a member of the Trinity Players and a good mimic. They were both in the School of Modern Languages and were a good contrast to the Medical School.

Three times a week students in college had to attend Night Roll. They donned their gowns and made their way to the Dining Hall, this time not to eat but to answer when the Junior Dean called out their names. This was to ensure that they passed the night in college and did not spend it roistering about the town. To this end the Junior Dean arrived in the company of two porters, one of whom carried a lamp. These precautions were taken after a Junior Dean had fallen into the darkness of a freshly dug pit. The latter part of this story is very likely apocryphal.

Some neighbours of ours in college asked us to join them on a shooting expedition. They lent me a gun and we set out in the dark before dawn. The plan was that we should drive to the head of Rogerstown inlet and there get out of the car and split into two groups. Two of us would walk down the bank of the inlet and climb onto the railway bridge, the others would then follow on down the inlet driving the wild geese from their roosts in the sea marsh, and which would then fly down over the railway bridge towards the sea and our waiting guns. Everything went according to plan until the geese approached the bridge, here they rose to a higher altitude, and passed high over us in the dawning light, well out of range. Not a shot was fired.

The geese disappeared over the sea and we met our friends again in the inlet. It had started to snow and we trudged back to the car. The fields and back roads became whiter as the snow accumulated. Eventually we reached the back gate of Trinity and parked behind the rugby pitch and walked round into New Square where we all lived in Number 40. The skip had lit a glowing fire and we had a memorable breakfast of kidneys, black pudding and eggs, quite forgetting the geese we didn't get.

Alice Graham (later known as Harry Bewick) in the 1920s

Alice Graham and Corbet Bewick on their wedding day

Harry Bewick: Friend and Future Mother-in-Law

The party was held in the spacious basement of a large townhouse on St Stephen's Green. The music, and it was quite noisy, was supplied by a gramophone which played seventy-eight RPM discs and which needed to be wound up quite often. Thus primed it emitted loud and accurate music. The date was in the early 1950s and the style of music was classical jazz. Most of the guests were young students who jived eagerly. In the centre of the room was an older woman, say in her forties or maybe even early fifties. She was with a group of attractive young people who clearly knew each other well, occasionally she herself danced with one of the young men. They dressed imaginatively and decoratively. I thought that they were perhaps a ballet group and that she was the ballet mistress.

I was in a group of students from Trinity who also knew each other well. Our group was male and the other group, mostly female. Naturally we mixed and a few of us were invited to visit their house the next day. We clambered into Mike Dawes' open sports car which gave a few booms and roars and arrived at a red brick Victorian house in Rathgar.

The sitting room was on the first floor and chairs were arranged with their backs to the walls. There was a brisk fire burning in the grate, and anyone wanting a chair just pulled one up to the fireside. The middle-aged woman turned out not to be a ballet mistress, but the owner of the house from which she let out inexpensive rooms. These enabled her, and her younger daughter Pauline, to live in Dublin where Pauline had enrolled in the National College of Art. The mother was known by her nickname and her married name: Harry Bewick. The nickname was bestowed when she fostered two Kerry children, the married name had been kept on when she parted from her husband.

Harry had lived in her native Tyneside with her two daughters Hazel and Pauline, together with her husband Corbet, in Batt Cottage. It is set amid trees and garden in the countryside near Corbridge. His family, the Bewicks, owned nearby Mickely Green Colliery and Corbet managed it. All sounds ideal, but in fact the marriage was perilous. Alice, as she was called at that time, was several years younger than Corbet and they hadn't learned to walk in step. Alice enjoyed going out with the miners for light-hearted gaiety. She also felt stifled by Corbet's mother, in particular objecting to the habit of cooking for her son and bringing meals back to Batt Cottage. This was all bad enough but then it became compounded by Corbet developing alcoholism.

Alice in her radical way decided that a complete break was the only remedy. She left everything behind, and took up the foster care of an orphaned brother and sister on a small farm in County Kerry. Harry, the change in name is emblematic, spent an idyllic six years with her daughters and the foster children. Tragically it was ended by the sudden death of Lucy from what was then called galloping consumption. Hazel, Harry's elder daughter, was approaching adolescence; she had always been a favourite of the Bewicks and inclined to rebel against her unconventional mother.

Now her beloved foster brother Michael was sent by his aunt to live in Switzerland for the sake of his health and so that he could learn the hotel trade. Harry had conceived the idea that she should travel around England taking the remaining children with her. They would attend progressive schools and she would work in them as a vegetarian cook – in my view, not her strongest suit.

Hazel dropped out of this and went to live in Northumbria with the Bewicks. This left Harry and Pauline: unafraid they tried various progressive schools, including the flower of the flock, Summerhill College, run by the inspirational A.S. Neill. Harry became disillusioned by institutional life and, encouraged by John Watling who became a lifelong friend, she gave up progressive schools.

At that time conventional houses were not for her and instead she bought a house-boat and journeyed in it through the Kennet and Avon Canal and moored it on the right bank of the Thames at Wargrave. Pauline was able to attend the elementary school from there and Harry must have had more leisure, at any rate she became an avid reader cutting her teeth on George Bernard Shaw, D.H. Lawrence, and Jiddu Krishnamurti.

Then there was her own book, *A Wild Taste*; it is a delight and should be read at least annually. There followed a peaceful interlude when Harry and Pauline moved into the Gate Lodge of the Cahernane Hotel, Killarney and in 1950 Pauline joined the Dublin Art School. It was at this juncture that, with the aid of a Building Society loan, Harry bought the house in Rathgar. She always joined in with Pauline and her chums' jollifications, and there were many parties at Fifty-One and round the town. Much as Harry enjoyed these youthful festivities, there were stronger forces in her life. Mention has already been made of her passion for reading and, in her next phase of life, this was joined by her love of nature, wild flowers, trees and natural history of all types. She bought a stone cottage at the back of Laragh School in Wicklow. It suited Harry very well. For heating she had turf and timber and in the summer there was Glenmacknass stream with the nearby Soldiers' Hole which was a delight for swimming.

Meals with Harry were informal occasions, she believed that they should be eaten out of the paper bags from which they were bought, thus eliminating the need for washing up.

There was a lot of laughter in the house. Much of it came from Harry and Pauline who both made loud raucous guffaws.

Harry was loved deeply by the ever-shifting inmates of Fifty-One, she was the friend we all wanted: irreverent, wise, experienced and tolerant.

Pauline Bewick and Pat Melia, c. 1952

Pat Melia and Pauline Bewick, c. 1952

Pat Melia and Pauline Bewick, c. 1952

On Killiney Strand, c. 1955

Pat, Pauline and Sesbatian Ryan, c. 1955

Paris by the Long Sea Route

It was summertime. Pauline, Harry and I sat about on the comfortable cushions on the low roofs of the back garden of 'Fifty-One', Harry's house in Rathgar. Pauline and I had decided that we really did not have enough money to go to Paris that summer. It was in the early fifties and forty pounds would have done it for the two of us. Neither of us had been to Paris before and neither of us had forty pounds. We would save up and go to Paris next year.

The following year found Pauline and I equipped with tickets for the mail boat which would take us from Dún Laoghaire to Holyhead. We lugged our suitcases up the narrow gangway aboard the powerful steamer and ensconced ourselves on deck where the two funnels towered above us. They emitted billows of steam and smoke and quickly whisked us away from the pier head and through the two arms of the Dún Laoghaire harbour piers onto Dublin Bay, passing close to the kish lightship. Speed was the essence. The mail train for London must not be delayed. It would speed through Anglesea passing the surprisingly named Welsh village that is spelled something like: Llanfairpull gwinceriogclantisiliogogogh. Then over the Menai Straites suspension bridge, and faster again it would head for London Euston.

Here we left the train and broke our journey making our way to Thurloe Place where we stayed with John Watling in his roomy flat opposite the Victoria and Albert Museum. The plan was to take the most economical way to our destination, and so we took the long sea route from Newhaven to Dieppe. Our friend David Brown informed us that this was known as The Pauper's Route. It was also bound for Paris and was going the same way as ourselves. We sat up on deck, a gentle breeze was blowing up the Channel and occasionally we were splashed by the spray. Soon we were lugging our increasingly irrelevant suitcases onto the quay at Dieppe, admiring the fresh Atlantic fish piled up there. We caught the Paris train and eventually saw in the distance the spires of Sacré Cœur, white and diminished like a tiny toy. In what seemed no time we were disgorged onto the platform at St Lazare amid the bustle of trolleys and suitcases. A large notice read: NE BUVEZ PAS PLUS QUE UN LITRE ET DEMI DU VIN PAR JOUR.

I had read about a small hotel, the Vieux Colombier which I thought would suit us perfectly in the Quatier Latin, inexpensive but comfortable. We took a taxi to it. I had not booked a room thinking that it would not be necessary, but the

Vieux Colombier had ceased to let out rooms. Crestfallen, we traipsed across the road opposite and spied a small hotel. Here on the first floor we were able to get a double room. Pauline was quick to unpack her drawing materials and a tiny set of watercolours; that done, she spread our travelling rug over the bed and instantly the room looked homely. The street was quite narrow and there were old-fashioned lace curtains.

Our first excursion was motivated by appetite. We were growing hungry and ventured out into the Rue de Dragon, the little street where we had discovered our hotel the night before. We joined the crowd in the Quatier Latin and picked out a small restaurant whose sign announced Le Polidor. We went in and took seats on one of the benches and read the menu. The waitress came quickly and took our orders; Radis Beurre followed by asparagus for Pauline; Salade de Tomates, followed by Cervelles Frites for me. With gusto the waitress banged down the food and wine at our places and we ate it with great enjoyment.

Next day we awoke refreshed, got dressed into light summer clothes to match the day and set off along the Rue du Dragon and soon came to the Boulevard St Germain. We turned right and came to a pleasantly proportioned old church set on one side of the busy Place St Germain des Prés. We crossed the road and found a table at the Café Deux Magots, which was comfortable, had a good view and was rather expensive. The coffee and croissants were excellent.

The sky was blue, the sun shone brightly and it was already warm. We bought the makings of a picnic lunch and set off on foot along the Left Bank of the Seine. Following directions given to us by John Latham, a friend back in Dublin, we came into a view of the Eiffel Tower. We struck down to a big floating barge which was moored to the bank. It contained a floating open swimming pool full of clear water and here we spent most of the day swimming and sunbathing.

Artists' materials were very much cheaper and more varied in Paris than in Dublin and Pauline took the opportunity of stocking up in the artists' shops round about the Rue Bonapart in St Germain de Près. While she was on one such expedition in the Rue St Jacob I went off to the English bookshop on the Left Bank opposite Notre Dame and was able to buy a copy of D.H. Lawrence's *Lady Chatterley's Lover*. This was an exciting achievement in itself because the book was banned in Ireland. I took it off to the terrasse of a café at the bottom of the Boulevard St Michel and there in the mild sunshine opened some of the uncut pages and realised that Pauline and I would have great pleasure in reading it aloud. And so we did. It seemed to me an extremely well-written novel with a succinct plot and interesting characterization of the two main protagonists, Lady Chatterley and the gamekeeper, Mellors. The straightforward treatment of sexuality is splendid and at the time it was written, daring. We made another trip to the bookshop to buy something else not obtainable in Dublin, *Tropic of Cancer*, by Henry Miller, but found it disappointing, and regretted trading in our copy of Lady Chatterley to fund its purchase.

Not very far from the Place Saint Germain de Près another excursion brought us to the Rue du Buci. Here several small streets converge and there is a street market. At it we bought cheese, saucissous, baguettes, fruit eau mineral and vin ordinair and made our way down the Rue de Seine, not lingering too long at the fascinating shop windows on account of our gastronomic burdens. Eventually we came to the river and crossed it by the Pont des Arts looking at the superlative view up-river where the arms of the Seine region and the towers of Notre Dame dominate the Île de la Cité. We climbed down the steps to the Quai du Louvre where we sat down and looked across the Seine at the river traffic. It mostly consisted of long narrow *péniches* whose open holds were filled with grain. In the deck-houses, well to the stern were the barges' captain and his family; cocks strutted about on the piles of grain, cats sunned themselves, and with the dogs, ensured that no unwelcome visitors jumped aboard. We spread our napkins on the warm quay and had our picnic.

For transport we preferred the metro or walking, though occasionally we stood on the open rear platform of the bus. One morning we took the metro as far as the end of the Louvre and from there walked past the Orangerie and across the Tuileries Gardens to the Jeu de Paume. Here we entered the building and mounted the steps. As we ascended, each step brought more of the inner wall in front of us into view with a flowing blaze of colour, and as we grew nearer we recognised the familiar Impressionists in this stupendous setting. A smaller work in the larger setting which delighted us was a chair sculpted in wood by Zadkine in the Musée d'Art Modern.

Although we had been disappointed by not finding lodging in the Vieux Colombier it so happened that we had an exciting visit to the nightclub there. Sidney Bechet had been booked in to play in the basement for the summer months. We arrived early while Claud Luter and his supporting band were playing. This was the cue for one and all to dance as they wished. Pauline and I jived away and were influenced by Catherine Dunham and her West Indian group who had visited Dublin a few months earlier.

There was a minor commotion at the back of the room. It was caused by the arrival of Bechet and his beautiful companion, a black woman wearing a woolen dress. They were escorted to a side table and a bottle of champagne was opened for them. The woman took out a swizzle stick and twirled it about in Bechet's glass. Pauline told me that it was to collect the bubbles so that they would not be too fizzy. Bechet carried his green sparkling soprano saxophone with him and mounted the shallow stage, immediately filling the room with quintessential jazz, rhythmic and sinuous with a tone quite distinct from anyone else. It was still ringing in our ears long after we had got back to the Hôtel du Dragon.

A Visit to the South

I woke early after an uneasy night's sleep, waking as our darkened compartment thundered and swayed speeding through the night. I stepped out into the corridor, the black darkness had gone, instead there was a twilight vision and a barren, mountainous landscape which grew brighter by the minute as the sun rose. Then there was the noise of banging doors and clattering crockery and a steward came around with black coffee. Pauline joined me from her slumber and we endured the now harsh sunlight as we sped towards the Mediterranean. It was our first experience of leaving our soft green temperate land and we sat tight until we reached St Raphael where we left the train and changed onto a bus bound for St Tropez, which was not yet a populous destination.

The bus ground along its road and came to rest behind some sheds where we surrendered our tickets. We picked up our bags and made our way towards some sunlit areas climbing a hill behind them and looking back on the shimmering waters of the harbour. We came to a gap between the houses and there was a pleasant building on which was painted: ALBERGO TROUPOLENCO. We got a room, no running water, but a basin and ewer. We rested and then got up and explored the village. We did what all the population appeared to be doing. One half walked to the end of the pier, while the other half walked back. The pace of the walk was leisurely and gave ample opportunity for the whole population to observe and greet each other. We found ourselves a table overlooking the harbour and inspected the unfamiliar menu. I plunged for triglia which turned out to be a fish with red flesh, and it tasted good. Pauline elected for ratatouille which was a vegetable stew and the carafe of chilled vin rosé was excellent. We walked around the harbour under the big sparkling stars, and like most of the other inhabitants of St Tropez in those days, went to bed early.

Breakfast was not served at the Albergo Troupolenco and we took the short walk down to the harbour and chose a table in the morning sunshine for our café au lait and croissants. A quick visit back to the Troupolenco to ready ourselves for the day and we set off in a westerly seaward direction which brought us onto higher ground above the village. We came out over the necropolis and walked still westward through a wood overtaking a tortoise and descending to a small sandy bay. There was a little café at its head. The water was a clear blue, varying to turquoise. We stationed ourselves on a little knoll near the head of the bay and made ourselves comfortable.

The bay was ideal for swimming, quite soon one was in deep water and it was pleasant to look out beyond the little cove at the mountains in the distance.

A year has passed and we have decided to explore the south more widely and that the way to do it is on our newly-acquired motor scooter. It is a 150cc Peugeot with a little platform over the front mudguard which can be used for stowing luggage. To give ourselves a good start we will put the machine in the train's luggage van as far as Milan and that will put us within striking distance of Italy's Riviera di Ponente and the Riviera di Levante.

We are in the railway station at Milan waiting for the scooter to arrive off the train, but there is no sign of it. At the information office we are advised to catch a train to Turin and pick up the scooter the next day. A sleepy hotelier shows us a room. She warns us to keep the window closed, and chases out a large tabby cat.

Next morning we made our way back to the station and there leaning on a wall was the scooter quite unattended, having got there as mysteriously as it had disappeared the day previously. We accepted it as mana from the skies.

Pat Melia outside the Rotunda Hospital
(2nd row from back, far left)

Pat outside St Patrick's Hospital, Dublin

BEGINNING MEDICINE

After a few years leading a life approaching that of a dilettante it seemed that I must engage more closely with the study of medicine. The first two subjects that I encountered were medicine itself, and surgery. We started with the morning clinic at which about a dozen of us accompanied the clinician on his morning round. We would halt at the bedside of one of the patients and he would demonstrate the points of interest of the case. This went on at one of the Trinity Hospitals. The students would choose which hospital they liked and attend whichever clinician they pleased. The Trinity teaching hospitals were Sir Patrick Dunn's; the Royal City of Dublin Hospital, known colloquially as Baggot Street; the Adelaide; and Mercers Hospital.

I threw in my lot with Baggot Street. Most of the literary people were there, and both the Professor of

Medicine, Victor Millington Synge; and Professor of Surgery, Jack Henry, were there.

Professor Synge was a scholarly and kind man. His enjoyment of his work was infectious and he had an extensive entourage of junior doctors following him on his rounds. He was amused to allude to them as his amanuenses.

In the course of time I became one of his House Physicians. He was incidentally the nephew of John Millington Synge, the famous writer. The Professor of Surgery, Jack Henry, was a different kettle of fish entirely. He conducted his clinic with flamboyance. One of the students would be commanded to take the floor and would be ironically addressed as 'doctor' – 'Now doctor step forward into the arena'. This was the ring of students around the bedside where his knowledge would be tested. If it were found wanting the student would be subjected to a tirade of scorn which would at the same time impress a number of surgical principals in the class and somehow no-one made objection to his insults.

Baggot Street Hospital was situated in an area of broad tree-lined streets, but itself was an ugly red-brick neo-Victorian affair. I reached it by a ride on my new motor scooter from Rathgar which tapped its way over the concrete slabs of Waterloo Road. Here I dismounted and made for the Junior Doctors' Mess and at the side table helped myself to an ample breakfast. Thus fortified I went to the wards. These were built on the open plan system and in the centre of each ward was a table on which there were arranged measuring jars, one for each patient, all containing a generous specimen of urine. The junior doctors' job was to test the urine for abnormal substances, and numerous chemical reagents were put on the tables for this purpose. The simplest way was just a matter of filling a test tube partially full of the patient's urine, then tilting it at approximately forty-five degrees and holding it over a flame. If the heated urine became cloudy it indicated that it contained albumen and that the patient needed further investigation and treatment.

It was now time to catch up with the consultant and do a round with him in order to see all the patients together and make notes on their management and treatment. Once a week we saw out-patients and there were special clinics for such groups as diabetic patients and such like. At lunch time there was usually a group of stragglers who were slow to come to the table and the hospital domestic, Nellie, would round them up, bellowing, 'Hey Synge! Let them in out of that to have their dinners'.

Somehow Nellie was always at the top of the hierarchy. Even when she had her tonsils out she was placed in a single room in the private wing.

After turning it over in my mind for quite a while I decided that it was not just a passing whim but that I should study Psychiatry. I wrote to Dr J.N.P. Moore, the Medical Superintendent at St Patrick's Hospital in Dublin, and after a while received a reply to the effect that there were no vacancies on the staff. Somewhat abashed I turned to the jobs vacant section of the *British Medical Journal* and soon found a position as Junior Hospital Medical Officer at Tooting Bec Hospital in South London.

Two thousand older people found their last home here and it was my job to look after the medical needs of six hundred of them. The nursing staff were most attentive and affectionate to the patients and my role was secondary.

The hospital was vast and rambling and was built on the villa system; numerous pavilions were separated by trees and gardens. It was originally intended for epileptics, but it was decided that the need for housing demented patients was greater. Several estates, such as the Horton and West Park estates were amalgamated and London's senile dements were accommodated in their place.

At first I lived in a flat in Regent's Park and later moved in with Barry Laverty and Philip Castle. Despite the name Barry was female. I usually ate out at a basement restaurant in Soho, known variously as The Greek, or Jimmie's. It was run by a Greek Cypriot family. The food was ample and robust. The menu was recited to the customers 'Chickens, Livers, Lamb Chop, Pork Chop, Chips, Salad, French Beans' and I brought in my own bottle of beer from the off-licence upstairs.

After two years as a Junior Hospital Medical Officer at Tooting Bec I became Psychiatric Registrar at St Ebba's Hospital at Epsom. I was enrolled in the Institute of Psychiatry and this was based at the Maudesley Hospital for Psychiatry and Queen Square Hospital for Neurology. I introduced a little unrecognised variant of my own into the weekly day release course by recording and analyzing my own dreams, using the psychoanalytical model. After two years I returned to Ireland.

At this point I was busy with clinical practice and with clinical teaching, both post-graduate and under-graduate. One morning Dr Moore told us at a staff meeting that there was a paper recently published by Cade, an Australian author, suggesting that lithium, taken daily, was capable of preventing the episodes of mood disorder which characterize manic depressive disorder. I had in fact already read the paper and did not attach very much importance to it.

Dr Moore thought otherwise and pointed out that recurrent affective disorders accounted for a significantly large proportion of re-admissions to psychiatric hospitals at that time and asked me to look closely through the literature. This I did and became intrigued by what was known about Bipolar Disorder and lithium use in psychiatry. It has become, and at the time of writing remains, the standard treatment for Bipolar Disorder.

Pauline and I got married in January 1963. I gave up my job after two years at St Ebbas and we went off in our tiny open sports car and made for the Alps to spend the next four months in those regions.

On our return we moved to Dublin. 17 Heytesbury Lane was a mews house which shared a garden with the front house and it was there that we bought the little house which became our Dublin home. We knocked an extra window looking south over the gardens up to the Dublin mountains. Indeed light became a premium as Pauline used the big room upstairs as a studio.

Then came Poppy in 1966, followed by Holly in 1970. There were home helps: Madge came from County Wicklow, her sandwiches were the best ever. She was followed by the even younger Theresa, a top class comedian.

Poppy and Pat in Heytesbury Lane

The babies, Poppy and Holly, seemed to me the most precious things I had ever seen. I suppose this is a phenomenon that ensures the survival of the species. Holly was full of ebuliant humour which could alternate with temper to the extent that earned her the nickname Thunderball, but it was soon over. Poppy, on the other hand, was calm and sensible and wise beyond her years.

Our next move was another step towards the country and its inhabitants. It took us further than the step from London to Dublin. The gulf between

Dublin and Kerry was like crossing to another continent. First the accent was so impenetrable that I could hardly understand anything that was said to me. After six months I could make out some of the words, but then, although I could distinguish the words, they did not seem to make any sense to me. Despite this the patients expressed great satisfaction with their treatment. I worked at Killarney Hospital and at out-patient clinics throughout the county in the Kerry Psychiatric Service.

Pat and Holly, Milltown, County Kerry, 1971

The medical staff included the Coroner and Ursula, a young American graduate. The Coroner was a local General Practitioner who had a part-time affiliation to the psychiatric service and a wealth of anecdotes concerning local happenings. Ursula in fact had only come back from the United States twelve months previously and her American accent was slipping away from her and being replaced by a Kerry lilt. Each Friday we set off from Killarney in my car; Ursula, Sean O'Connor, the Community Nurse, and I. Sean O'Connor preferred the title Community Lad to Community Nurse which I think he thought effeminate. We went to Listowel where the out-patient clinic was held. On the way out one day Sean O'Connor was in full spat. Ursula had not yet spoken a word but suddenly in a side field she spied two donkeys copulating which made her call out 'ooh! look!'

On another occasion Sean escorted a research worker, Lelia, together with the little child whom she was breastfeeding, in the district. He was astonished at the little girl's appetite and described her suckling so vigorously that two streams of milk ran down the baby's face, one either side of her nose. To top it all when the baby had finished suckling, Lelia held it out over the oil cloth and the baby urinated liberally over the floor.

Poppy, Pat, Holly and Theresa Doyle in Tuscany

Pat, Holly and Poppy in Paris, 1975

Seán Mac Reamoinn, Maria Simmonds-Gooding,
Pat and Holly, Kerry, c. 1982

The family in Tuscany and Treanmanagh

SMALL CAR TO TUSCANY

I was sitting in my room in the Student Health Service office in Trinity preparing a lecture on the Irish personality with one aspect of the latter impinging on my concentration. It was a few days after Bloody Sunday when troops had fired on unarmed demonstrators in Derry, and the previous night an enraged crowd had stormed and burned the British Embassy in Fitzwilliam Square. Now their angry shouts filled the air and could be heard as far away as the Student Health rooms in Botany Bay, Trinity College, Dublin. I cannot remember the content of my lecture nor can I find the notes which I made, only the title.

My wife Pauline Bewick is a well-known painter and we had two little girls. The tragic discord of that time was distressing and we had a long-standing invitation to borrow a dilapidated vacant farmhouse in the hills of Tuscany. I suggested that I should take my annual leave and that we should decamp immediately.

We packed up our luggage in suitcases and secured them to the roof-rack of our white Renault 4. This was an excellent little car: lightweight with, I think, an 850 cc engine, four doors and an estate car door at the back where we packed the picnic things. This left the four seats for our family: usually I drove ensconced behind the amber-coloured steering wheel; Pauline sat in front frequently dispersing little snacks of such things as raisins and apples; behind her was Poppy about five years old; and behind me, Holly, about one year old and not yet able to walk or talk, but nevertheless able to assert imperious territorial rights over her eiderdown cover and the air-space above it. We were all on our best behaviour; the enormity of our journey somehow communicated itself even to the most junior members of our little party.

We emerge from our cabin and step out onto the after-deck of the Dublin-Liverpool ferry. We are passing out of Dublin Bay. It is snowing great wet flakes; the Bailey Lighthouse, Howth Head behind and above it and spread out astern the twinkling lights of Dublin Bay. The snow is already a few inches deep on the deck and the wind is dark and chilly. Some stars are out behind the falling snow lakes. We have a last look around before making back for our cabin.

We disembark next morning at Liverpool. There is the murmur of talk in the Custom House shed as the customs men rummage in our cases. I apologize for not having anything of interest and they laugh. We stop the car as soon as we are outside the customs' buildings. The Liver Building looms over us. We look at the map. We will take the motor-way towards Manchester as far as the junction with the M6 and there turn south for London.

Midway between Liverpool and Manchester we are passing through deserted countryside when the car's little engine begins to labour and we lose speed, the wind buffets the screen, and we go slower still. I decide to stop and investigate. I jump out, there is a stiff breeze against us and I notice that there is a gradient which we have been ascending. We are not used to this large scale: what we need is a lower gear. I jump back into the car, resisting the temptation to tack up the broad carriageway and instead motored on in a lower gear with the desired result.

We were going to stay overnight with Susan Godwin and Ted Hondrich, our friends. They live in their house at the foot of Hampstead Hill. Susan had lived together with us in 'Fifty-One' as Pauline's mother's house in Rathgar was colloquially called. Susan had studied Religion at Trinity. She wanted to understand it from the view of social psychology and became unique in Trinity's School of Divinity. Ted, immensely tall, a Canadian, was a lecturer in Philosophy at University College, London.

The children were in bed; we were relaxing after a cosy dinner and decided to look at the weather report. We were booked on a hovercraft to cross the Channel the next day. To our horror the television news showed us that the day had been very windy and that a hovercraft crossing the Solent to the Isle of Wight had flipped and capsized, throwing passengers into the sea. They could be plainly seen struggling to keep afloat and find something to hold onto, a nightmare scene. Eventually the program moved to another topic leaving us dumbfounded. What are we going to do tomorrow? What will the weather be like tomorrow? Will we be thrown into the sea to fight against the waves? A tumult of questions spoken and unspoken went through our minds and were discussed by us. Should we cancel our cross-channel tickets for the next day or not? Ted made numerous phonecalls to elucidate the situation, prefacing each with the grave announcement 'Hondrich here'.

Around most of the questions there grew a polarization of views: one school of thought argued that lightening does not strike the same place twice so that a repeat capsize could be discounted; another held that a weather pattern of high winds had been established and might well continue the next day making the sea dangerous. We asked Ted to phone again and cancel our hovercraft booking and get us a refund, leaving us free to decide what to do the next day, and kind and patient, he did that.

The next day was perfect, the barometer had risen, the sun had come out and the wind had dropped. We repacked the bulging R4, said 'goodbye' to our hosts and went off to Dover, resolved to catch the first boat to Calais. We arrived in Dover at the ferry port at the foot of the white cliffs. The sea was blue and I walked over to the booking office and booked us on the next ferry which ironically was a hovercraft. We had a swift, flat crossing and the hovercraft mounted the beach at Calais with smooth assurance. We took the road in a south-easterly direction towards Reims so that we would avoid the heavy traffic around Paris. After a while we spied a low house standing on its own, set back from the road, and bearing the sign CHAMBRES. The house was built around three sides of a square, with proverbial French windows opening to the central square. We took one wing of the house. It was quiet and comfortable and suited us perfectly.

Next morning we packed our overnight bags and set off on the road to Amiens and Reims and stopped at the first village that we came to and sat down for café au lait and croissants. Then Pauline went off to shop for the picnic lunch that we would have. She returned laden with good things: camembert, chevre, baguettes, fruit, saucisson, jambon, a bottle of red wine and eau minéral. These were stowed away and off we went bouncing over the road. At one o'clock we looked for a side road and soon found one with a grass margin and little evidence of traffic. We spread our rug and Pauline dispensed the delicious lunch.

We now entered the Champagne country and crossed the rolling hills, brown and bare apart from the dormant vineyards etched in the landscape awaiting spring.

Time to make an overnight stop. Reims looked too busy and we went on to quieter Epernay where we found a pleasant hotel. We took a *grande-chambre de famille* in which there was room for us all. Pauline heated some milk for Holly and elected to stay in the room and finish the lunch-time picnic and have an early night as she had a headache. Poppy and I went out to a nearby restaurant. Poppy had *poulet rôti avec pommes frites*. I had something much the same except that it was covered with the local specialty: champagne sauce.

We all slept well, Pauline's headache was gone and we were served breakfast in our room. The morning's copy of *Le Figaro* was folded on the breakfast tray and I had the luxury of reading the headlines before getting up and dressing. The children were still entranced by the novelty of life aboard the R4 and went about with broad smiles on their faces. Pauline and I did our morning chores: she the picnic provisions, I the car servicing, filling up with petrol, checking the oil, putting it through the carwash, deciding on the route, writing it down in capital letters, and sticking it on the dashboard.

<u>ROUTE</u>
EPERNAY
CHAUMONT
LANGRES
DIJON
BEAUNE
MACON
LYON
MONTELEMAR
ORANGE
AVIGNON
AIX EN PROVENCE

After our picnic lunch, a leisurely affair, we motored on. The vineyards of Champagne were soon left behind and we descended the valley of the Saône and then the valley of the Rhône. Big grey clouds filled the sky and the light faded early. Pauline lit the spirit lamp to heat Holly's milk, it flared up momentarily and filled the room with light and then died down again.

Next day we motored through Provence and made for the little port at Villefranche-sur-Mer, which Pauline and I knew from earlier visits. The R4 lumbered down the steep hill from the Route-Nationale in a low gear. We parked in front of the Hotel de la Darse near to the spot where we had painted and anti-fouled the *Carn Ingli* ten years previously. We were all ravenous and as soon as we could we made off for a waterside restaurant and noisily made our orders, the grown-ups helping the children.

The following day, the last day of the journey, we packed rapidly, perhaps too rapidly. It was Poppy's birthday, March the ninth and we forgot her new bunny rabbit hot-water bottle in the bottom of her bed. There were heartbreaking tears, but eventually good humour was restored. We were getting near to the end of our journey and the landscape had changed as we skirted the southern fringes of Florence. We were now gradually climbing up the Val d'Arno and around us were terraces stretching in every direction. The olive trees were old, gnarled and twisted by heavy pruning. The pruners had left fresh-looking smaller branches bearing new silvery leaves. It was too early to see the tiny new olives which were still to come. The vines were trained on poles between the old trees so that the olives and grapes would grow mingled together.

Philip and Barry had given us a clear simple sketch-map showing the way from village to village through terraces and fields until we came to their casa colonica. A casa colonica is a colony of small houses clustered together, built by the landlord for his tenant farmers. Philip and Barry used theirs as a summer house and artists' studio which they were lending to us while they were in England.

It was growing dark and there was a driving sleet blowing across the front of the house. We walked around the back and discovered a dimly-lit window. There was the sound of voices inside and I tapped on the glass. The voices stopped and after a silence were replaced by the rattle of keys. The door opened on a small party having tea and cakes. It was a Sunday afternoon treat in the 'cantina'. Parigi who was in charge produced a bunch of keys which served our part of the casa: the kitchen and a bedroom on the ground floor, and two more bedrooms on the floor above and a narrow staircase which led to a box-like skylight in which there lived a family of barn owls. Facing the door was an enormous stone fireplace, and here we lit a fire, using scraps of timber lying about the place. We bedded down in the kitchen listening to the cluck of hens and the snorting of pigs coming from we were not sure where. By now it was quite dark, but we had candles and torches and made ourselves comfortable; the children were delighted by the animal and bird noises and we went to sleep.

Next morning the weather had effected another transformation. The sky was blue, the day felt warm and the green field in front and above the house was full of wild calendula flowers. Barry and Philip's map had been accompanied by a booklet of information which they had written and which was a very useful survival kit and reference book. We sat down in the 'campo' amongst the flowers and took in the scene. The 'campo' was set in a mixed olive grove and vineyard sloping down in front of us. Beyond was a wood of oak and chestnut trees and a valley, ranges of hills on top of which were houses and more olive groves. It was all a delight.

There were a couple of local skills to be mastered: opening the front door; the key was immense and worked by sweeping it across the key hole rather than by rotating it; the other was drawing water from the well. This was easy. The important thing was to keep the bucket and chain always inside the well, bolted to the inner roof of the well where they kept themselves clean and cool, better than throwing them down heedlessly; upon the dusty, hot paving stones around the well and using them again unrinsed on the next visit to the well.

The weather was set fair and we went to Siena and walked down the medieval terracotta brick town to the magnificent Piazza del Campo where the elegant Sienese strolled in their long brick coloured overcoats, which to our Nordic bodies seemed unnecessarily warm on that sunny day.

There were two families at Bricciano with farms. Gigi and Caterina's son had grown up and was a gamekeeper and Gigi continued the farm work. He had two white oxen and brought them for special work, such as getting in the hay. The other family was the Rossis; Bruna, her husband Piero, and Gino, Piero's brother.

All were very friendly, and Poppy in particular became a constant companion of Caterina and Bruna. They kept rabbits in a row of little hutches and each day Poppy would help, gathering grass and herbs to bring in to them. Bruna and Caterina kept in touch by calling across the little valley in a pleasant sing-song way.

Every once in a while we would have a *merenda,* which was a picnic. Lots of neighbours would come and food and wine would be brought and spread out on a long table. I was always seated next to the priest, Don Lilliano, who was most jovial. We conversed in the few bits of language that we had in common, including Latin, and managed to have quite wide-ranging conversations. The senese were very friendly and talkative especially with the children, and always enquired was Holly 'bimbo' or 'bimba'.

On our first visit to Siena for lunch we chose one of the restaurants on the Piazza terrace and placed Holly in the middle of the back row where she stood on her chair and had a good view down the scallop-shaped piazza. We tied the white linen napkin around her neck and she ate her red spaghetti napolitana heartily with the big silvery fork and perhaps her own hands too.

If the weather was not good Poppy occupied herself by 'making things'. This consisted of collecting large pieces of cardboard and snipping and bending and modelling and pasting until she made whatever it was that she wanted, and she showed great ingenuity in this. She was the elder daughter and wise before her time. Even Pauline or I would ask her opinion on quite grown-up matters.

When the summer ended we all returned to Dublin to resume our careers. Pauline recorded the stay in Tuscany with an exhibition which was shown with great success at the Italian Embassy in Dublin.

Pat with his former student Professor Anthony Clare launching Pauline's exhibition in London 1987

Pat and family on the South Seas, 1989

Conor (Poppy's husband), Pat, Holly, Matteo (Holly's stepson), Luca (Holly's husband), Poppy and baby Aran in Austria, 1998

With Charles and Elizabeth Handy, 1999

Galloping Across Slovenia

I was buying my morning newspaper in New Street, Killarney when I was confronted by the picture on the front cover of a country magazine. It showed, in profile, the head of a big handsome white horse whose expression was at once alert and placid. I bought the magazine immediately and on reading it learnt that the horse was a Lipizzaner. These are the renowned dressage horses of the Spanishereitschule at Vienna. But that is not all: one must know something of their history in order to fully appreciate them. They originate from the Arab horses of North Africa and were brought to Europe via Spain. The breeding stock was built up on a half dozen or so Andalucian stallions. These were bred with the local working mares from around Lipica, in the same way as the early English thoroughbreds were the progeny of Arab stallions and English and, perhaps Irish, draught mares.

This was the time of the Renaissance and a sumptuous stud was built for the Andalucians with their flowing manes and tails, and their tough, hard-working, good-natured consorts. This was at Lipica, which is the Slovenian version of Lipizza (hence Lipizzaner), where the original Renaissance buildings are still in daily use.

At the end of World War I the stud was split and one half went to Austria at Piber taking with it the Spanishereitschule; while the original stud remained in Slovenia. Both studs produced the famous white horses which are brown at birth and remain so until they are aged around four, at which time they gradually, like some of us humans, turn grey, and then white. They are fine healthy animals and live to a good age.

Lipica is a large estate on wooded rolling parkland. The Renaissance stud has three main buildings as well as a beautiful baroque chapel, which, when I visited, was in disuse except to house used empty cardboard boxes and the like. The other buildings are old, elegant, long and low. One is for the mares and foals; the second for the dressage horses; and the third houses the riding stables; and there is also a modern hotel for visitors, and I booked to stay there.

My main interest was to ride the legendary Lipizzaners on cross-country expeditions. These were held every few days, and between times there were rides across the demesne, and that is what I did the first day. I was given a fine horse, a gelding of about sixteen hands, attentive and responsive. His name was something like (the intervening years may have blurred my memory) Favory Steaka XXII.

Favory indicates the stallion line and steaka the native mare. Favory Steaka was obviously well schooled but was not going to be put upon. I gave him a tap with the whip each time we began to canter. He replied with a discreet buck – point taken, there was no need to tap him, and after this we got on very well together, and I was delighted when I was told that he was to be my mount the following day on a cross-country ride.

First on the move each morning were the mares and foals. They crossed the demesne rapidly with on air of exuberance and the grooms cracked their whips to round up any stragglers so that the dark foals and their white mothers moved like a rapidly flowing river across the demesne.

Knots of riders walked to the dressage halls with serious and thoughtful expressions. I made for the riding stables. There was a cheerful atmosphere of suppressed excitement as the horses were led out. Favory Steaka was in the van and one of the stable girls handed me the reins and I led him to a quiet spot in order to mount. Walking beside him I could not see over his withers and I realized that I would need a leg up. Everyone was busy, so I took him to a small fence and climbed on it to get a leg over him.

The leader of our group called on us to start and off we went through the demesne towards the Eastern Gate. Our object was to ride to a village about twenty miles away in the morning, have lunch there and ride back in the afternoon, after resting the horses and ourselves.

We set off through the little village clustered outside the gate. Favory Steaka took a lively interest in his surroundings, peering over garden walls where often he saw a mare grazing on the back lawn, and down each side lane he saw groups of mares. Soon we were on rising ground, with pastures dotted with limestone rocks typical of this karst country. The horses avoided the stones, effortlessly lengthening and shortening their strides as necessary, used to it all their lives. We passed a group of wrecked cars, a flock of sheep was being herded, and a party of hawks was soaring around.

Ahead of us lay rock outcrops in the conifer forest, and higher were bare hills. We came to a ridge from which we saw a series of hilly ranges between which there were little valleys of cleared pastures in which the turf was soft and springy. In the far distance was a Venetian-style church-tower and dome that marked our destination. As on most of the continent there were very few hedges and ditches. Grazing animals were frequently kept in enclosures or tended by herders, which suited cross-country riders very well. We came down off the ridge to the floor of the valley, the horses and riders getting more and more excited; first sitting-trots, then giving the horses their heads, rising out of the saddles and off at a gallop, hell for leather up the valley. Two horses stumbled and fell. One close to Favory Steaka who skipped sideways. I managed to keep my seat and the two fallen riders were soon up again. On we went, Favory Steaka enjoyed the gallop and we pulled out from the rear of the group and moved up with the leaders, keeping well on the outside. This position had the disadvantage of being over rather rough ground but Favory Steaka could manage it and we had a clear run. The valley led into a laneway which brought us into the village. We trotted up to the inn where we dismounted, tethered our horses, and took off their steaming saddles.

We strolled around to the front of the inn and saw that the long tables were laid for lunch. As we sat down we saw that by each place there was a small glass of what proved to be slivovitz placed on the left of our plates. We were told that this was the custom and that we must drink it down straight away in one swallow. This we did and there followed an immediate loosening of tongues and feeling of bonhomie.

After an excellent lunch most of us found a shady tree and slept or dozed until it was time to tack up the horses ready for the ride back to Lipica.

This was a much more relaxed affair than the ride out. The tense expectancy was replaced by jollity. Gradually the sun sank in the west and we were riding into it, dazzled by its slanting rays until it set and we rode into the demesne as dusk was falling.

Pat and a Maori in New Zealand, 2000

Pat, Pauline, Sydney, Nina, Poppy, Easkey, Mike and Regine in Ballymaloe House, 2005

Pat and Pauline, c. 2010